The Werewolf

Monsters
and Mythical Creatures

The Werewolf

Kris Hirschmann

ReferencePoint
Press®

San Diego, CA

© 2012 ReferencePoint Press, Inc.
Printed in the United States

For more information, contact:
ReferencePoint Press, Inc.
PO Box 27779
San Diego, CA 92198
www.ReferencePointPress.com

LIBRARY OF CONGRESS CATALOGING-IN-PUBLICATION DATA

Hirschmann, Kris, 1967–
The Werewolf / by Kris Hirschmann.
    p. cm. -- (Monsters and mythical creatures)
Includes bibliographical references and index.
ISBN-13: 978-1-60152-238-2 (hardback)
ISBN-10: 1-60152-238-X (hardback)
1. The Werewolf--Juvenile literature. I. Title.
GR830.W4.H57 2012
398.24'54--dc23
                                                                2011036347

Contents

Introduction

From Man to Beast

But, lo! what awful change is taking place in the form of that doomed being? His handsome countenance elongates into one of savage and brute-like shape; the rich garments which he wears become a rough, shaggy, and wiry skin; his body loses its human contours, his arms and limbs take another form; and, with a frantic howl of misery, to which the woods give horribly faithful reverberations, and, with a rush like a hurling wind, the wretch starts wildly away, no longer a man, but a monstrous wolf![1]

This vivid passage was written in the late 1800s. Modern readers, however, are certain to recognize the creature it portrays. The author is describing the werewolf, a half-human, half-animal monster that has stalked people's nightmares for thousands of years. This beast appears in the legends of practically every culture and every time period since the beginning of written history. Its traits differ a little from one place to another, but the essential idea is always the same: Certain men and women, at certain times, can physically

Few, if any, people have witnessed the bizarre physical transformation from human to werewolf. Still, vivid descriptions nevertheless prevail in stories from long ago, as well as in modern tales. Contemporary writers, filmmakers, and others give ongoing life to the image of the werewolf prowling beneath the full moon.

change into wolves. This change may be voluntary or involuntary—but either way, it is always dangerous to the people nearby.

Historical records show that the perceived danger varies in different traditions. In ancient Greece, for example, werewolves were important mythological figures, but it seems they were not taken very seriously in real life. In medieval Europe, on the other hand, wolf-humans were thought to be everywhere. Thousands of French and English citizens were arrested, tried, and even executed for allegedly being werewolves during the 1500s and 1600s. Other parts of Europe, too, are rife with werewolf tales—not surprising, perhaps, for a time when real wolves posed an everyday danger to people and livestock.

Today wolves are not as common as they used to be, and it seems that werewolves have suffered the same fate. Although the belief in werewolves has not entirely disappeared, people in modern times tend to think of werewolves as fictional creatures. They may be good for chills and thrills around the campfire, but they pose no threat to those who are out at night.

Medical studies support this belief. Despite their best efforts, scientists cannot find any evidence that humans can physically shift into animal forms. They do acknowledge that some people *think* they change into wolves. They have even coined a term, *lycanthropy*, to describe this condition. Yet they do not believe any real transformation takes place.

Most people accept this reassuring view. Some people, though, are not so sure. They think maybe, just maybe, people really do turn into wolves. Maybe these creatures do

stalk nighttime walkers, and maybe it is best to stay inside when the full moon shines—just in case. There is no telling what terrible things might happen when werewolves are on the prowl.

Chapter 1

What Are Werewolves?

In the depths of the night, the countryside is quiet and still. Usually it is dark as well—but not on nights when the fields and woods are washed in the silvery light of a full moon. Riding high in a cloudless sky, the glowing orb shines brightly enough to cast shadows on Earth's slumbering surface.

The shifting shadows reveal movement at the edge of a nearby forest. A bush rustles as a creature emerges. At first glance the thing looks like a wolf. A closer inspection, however, reveals that the beast has glowing eyes unlike any normal animal. It is huge and hairy, and it gives off an air of barely re-strained fury.

It gives off something else as well. It is an impression, hard to define, that something is awry. The creature seems aware, somehow, in a way that animals should not be. It moves and behaves—strangely enough—like a human.

There is a good reason for this behavior. The creature *is* human most of the time. On this night, however, it is an animal. On this night it hunts. On this night the werewolf is on the loose.

A Beastly Transformation

This scenario presents a typical view of the werewolf—a monster that is part human, part beast, and all awful. It describes the way a werewolf looks and acts after its beastly transformation.

It is easy to summarize these traits. The classic werewolf appears much like a real wolf, with a few key differences. It is unusually big, strong, and fast compared to its wolf cousins. Its eyes may glow in the dark, and its fur may have a silvery sheen. The creature is smarter and more cunning than any natural animal. Most frightening of all, the werewolf is unfailingly vicious—and it is always hungry for human flesh. Any unlucky person who encounters this monster is virtually guaranteed to become its next meal.

These qualities define werewolves in the modern world. During other eras, however, people have had different views of the werewolf. In some traditions, for example, people believed that werewolves walked upright and had human or human-like bodies. Sometimes they even spoke and acted like humans. Only the heads of these creatures were wolf-like.

Some Christian scholars of the 1500s and 1600s had a different idea of the werewolf. The physical transformation from man to beast, they reasoned, was a miracle. Yet only God could perform miracles, and surely he would never create something as horrifying as a werewolf. Werewolves must, therefore, be the work of Satan. The devil was not as talented as God, though, so he always botched the job in some way. For this reason werewolves looked mostly like wolves, but with subtle differences. They might lack tails, for instance, or their body proportions might be awry. Some small deformity always betrayed Satan's imperfect handiwork.

Werewolves by Choice

The devil's work might have been shoddy, but according to centuries-old writings, many people longed to experience the hellish change anyway. They went to great lengths to earn werewolf powers.

Performing satanic rituals was one way to accomplish the deed. Ancient texts provided step-by-step instructions for these rituals. The instructions generally had to be carried out in a certain place at a certain time. For instance, the ceremony might need to take place in a forest at midnight under a full moon. Once these conditions or

Werewolf Hallucinations

At least one modern scholar believes that werewolves could be real—in their own minds, at least. Mary Kilbourne Matossian, a professor of history at the University of Maryland, has reviewed thousands of werewolf stories from the 1500s and 1600s. She has concluded that the so-called werewolves in these accounts were probably humans who had been poisoned by a natural substance called ergot.

Ergot is a fungus that attacks rye. Hundreds of years ago infected rye was often harvested and made into bread. If people ate this bread, they experienced a condition called ergotism. This malady could produce many symptoms, including psychosis and vivid hallucinations.

In her book *Poisons of the Past: Molds, Epidemics, and History,* Matossian explains how ergot-induced hallucinations could have contributed to a belief in werewolves.

> Some individuals . . . imagined themselves being transformed into animals, such as wolves. . . . The ergot caused them to act in other bizarre ways, even committing murder and injury. As a result, numerous victims of ergot poisoning were tried as wolves and werewolves—and executed. With the advent of modern methods of cleaning and processing grain, ergot was eliminated—along with the appearance of werewolves.

Mary Kilbourne Matossian, *Poisons of the Past: Molds, Epidemics, and History.* New Haven, CT: Yale University Press, 1989.

others were met, the would-be werewolf might have to draw magical symbols or mix potions and recite spells. If all of these steps were followed correctly, Satan would appear and perhaps grant the person's wish to be a werewolf.

After this deal was struck, the devil usually gave the new werewolf some type of magical implement. It might be a belt or a girdle. It might also be a pot of salve or directions for making the salve. It might even be a drinkable potion. Later the recipient could use these items to shift into wolf form at will. He or she might don the belt, for instance, or spread the salve all over the naked skin. Doing these things, in whatever way Satan instructed, was guaranteed to prompt the werewolf transformation.

According to some texts, all of these actions, plus a few others, were necessary. One author explains the requirements with these words: "Those who wish to become a werewolf [must] disrobe, rub a magical ointment freely over their flesh, place a girdle made of human or wolf skin around their waist, then cover their entire body with the pelt of a wolf. To accelerate the process, they should drink beer mixed with blood and chant a particular magical formula."[2]

The steps described in this excerpt are quite extensive. They show that becoming a werewolf was not something to take lightly. Rather, it was an occupation that required copious equipment, knowledge, and planning. Anyone could achieve werewolf status, but it took a lot of time and commitment to achieve this monstrous goal.

Werewolves by Birth

This was not the case for every werewolf. Far from seeking this beastly lifestyle, some people were dragged into it against their will. These people usually hated their wolfish natures. Scholar Sabine Baring-Gould explained this position in a classic 1865 text. "It must not be supposed that this madness or possession came only on those persons who predisposed themselves to be attacked by it," he wrote. "Others were afflicted with it, who vainly struggled against its influence, and who deeply lamented their own liability to be seized with these terrible accesses of frenzy."[3]

A person could become prone to these "frenzies" in several ways. The most common was simply to be born with werewolf tendencies.

This could happen by an accident of timing. Babies born on Christmas Eve, for example, were watched closely for signs of lycanthropy. It was thought that these babies were committing acts of blasphemy by arriving on Christ's special day. God would punish them with the werewolf curse unless they conducted themselves with unrelenting holiness.

The same was true of children fathered by priests. In the Roman Catholic tradition, priests are supposed to remain celibate throughout their lives. Their children, therefore, might be considered products of sin. In some times and places, such children were thought to bear the burden of their fathers' indiscretions. God turned them into werewolves as revenge against their inappropriate parentage.

Less blasphemous but equally telling was a baby's birth order. Being the seventh son in a line of sons, for instance, was considered a very bad sign in parts of South America. Boys born into this dangerous situation were doomed to become werewolves, or *lobizon*, when they reached their thirteenth birthdays. They would flee into the woods and stalk living prey, including humans, for the rest of their wretched lives.

Certain physical features were also thought to lead to life as a werewolf. Babies born with thin membranes, called cauls, on their heads or faces were strongly suspected of being werewolves. Overly hairy babies might also carry werewolf genes. As they grew, these children were watched closely for evidence of werewolf traits.

Werewolves by Accident

In general, "born" werewolves were fairly easy to handle. People knew what to expect from them. This meant they could keep their eyes open for signs of trouble. They could imprison, banish, or even execute the werewolf the moment things got out of hand.

The same was not true of people who became werewolves by accident. Accidental werewolves were people who picked up the werewolf curse sometime after birth. The affliction could hit anybody at any age, and this made it very hard to predict. Angry and often out of control, accidental werewolves were among the most feared of all monstrous beings. There were said to be a few ways to stumble

into the werewolf lifestyle. One way was simply to sleep outdoors under the light of the full moon. The person who made this mistake, particularly on a Friday, might not be fully human when he or she awoke.

Drinking werewolf-tainted water was another sure route to transformation. Thirsty travelers might unknowingly sip from streams where werewolves had bathed. They might also drink the water that had pooled in a werewolf's footprints. It is admittedly hard to imagine someone doing this. Yet according to werewolf lore, it did happen. When it did, a werewolf change was sure to follow.

The most foolproof way to become a werewolf, of course, was to be bitten or scratched by one. Although very few werewolf victims survived, those who did carried a terrifying poison in their veins. At first this poison caused no outward symptoms. Inside the body, though, it was slowly but surely doing its dreadful work. When conditions were right, the werewolf's victim would start to writhe, to howl—to change. In just minutes the man or woman would disappear, and the wolf would emerge.

Forced to Change

Accidental werewolves had no control over this process. When the time was right, they changed into animals whether they wanted to or not. Several conditions were thought to cause this shift.

Some people believed that strong emotions, especially rage, could kick off the werewolf transformation. Humans who carried the werewolf curse, therefore, had to stay calm at all times. If their self-control slipped, they might start shifting into wolf form.

The arrival of nighttime was also thought to be a factor. In many cultures werewolves were considered to be human by day, wolf by night. The change happened every morning and evening without fail. As soon as the sun dropped below the horizon, the unlucky werewolf would begin his or her transformation.

The most common werewolf trigger of all, of course, was the full moon. The light of this celestial body was said to exert an irresistible power on werewolves. Some traditions claimed that the effect occurred only on the actual night of the full moon. Others said that it occurred for several days or even a week around this period. Whatever the exact timing, the result was always the same. The reluctant werewolf became agitated as twilight neared and the dreaded moment approached. He or she knew that the curse would take over as soon as the moon appeared.

The connection between werewolfism and the full moon is not common in folklore. It is sometimes said to be a modern invention. A careful look at werewolf writings, however, shows that this link was identified as early as the 1200s. In a book called *Otia Imperialia*, an English folk writer named Gervase of Tilbury discusses this phenomenon. "One thing I know to be of daily occurrence among the people of our country . . . certain men change into wolves according to the cycles of the moon,"[4] he writes. The author goes on to relate the story of the unfortunate Raimbaud de Pouget, a knight who allegedly suffered from this condition.

The Werewolf Illusion

Gervase of Tilbury was sure that de Pouget and other werewolves underwent a true transformation from human to animal. In this belief, Gervase held to the prevailing views of his time. The vast majority of common folk believed that people could, indeed, undergo a physical change to assume wolf form.

Some people, however, scoffed at this idea. They thought that the transformation was an illusion and that werewolves only *thought* they were wolves. This theory was especially popular among churchmen of the 1500s and 1600s, who claimed that the devil was responsible for the horrible hallucination.

In the early 1600s a writer named Richard Verstegen described this view in the colorful words and spelling of the era: "The were-

Were-Creatures of Many Types

Werewolf tales and legends abound in parts of Europe where wolves were once common. In other lands and cultures, though, different were-beasts may be more typical. Just about every frightening, powerful animal has been tagged as a were-creature somewhere in the world.

Were-cats of various types are especially popular. In India, for instance, people tell tales of were-tigers. Africa is said to be home to were-lions and were-leopards. Likewise, South American folklore is rife with stories of vicious, powerful beasts called were-jaguars. Cruel and hungry, these human-jaguar monsters still make occasional modern-day appearances—or at least, people say they do.

Other were-creatures have been reported in Scotland. The Scottish coasts are home to many seals, so it is not surprising that the legends of this region concern human-seal hybrids called were-seals. Were-seals are known for entering into doomed relationships with humans. These relationships often produce magical children who continue the were-seal tradition. No such offspring have been reported from the were-hippo, a beast that crops up occasionally in African lore. One such monster was even reported in recent years. Authorities were allegedly asked to investigate, but they refused. They felt that it would hurt the government's reputation if officials took the claim seriously.

wolves are certaine sorcerers, who . . . do not only unto the view of others seeme as wolves, but to their owne thinking have both the shape and nature of wolves. . . . And they do dispose themselves as very wolves, in wurrying and killing, and moste of humaine creatures."[5] It is important to note in this description that both the werewolf and its victims experience the wolf illusion. The fact that the werewolf is not real, therefore, does not make the creature any less terrifying or any less deadly. The monster still hunts and kills, just as a real wolf would. Likewise, its human targets experience—or believe they do, at least—the beastly ravages of the werewolf's sharp claws and teeth.

Werewolf Possession

The illusion explanation satisfied many long-ago religious theorists. Others, however, felt it was all a bit far-fetched. They thought it was much more likely that werewolves were simply people who could send their spirits out of their bodies. These roaming souls could enter and possess the bodies of real wolves. Once in control, they could wreak as much havoc as they liked without fear of harm or detection.

This theory was not only easier for some people to believe, but it was also very handy for local authorities. It explained the fact that wolf attacks sometimes occurred even after an accused werewolf had been caught and confined. As writer Daniel Cohen says, "It was possible . . . for an evil person to be asleep in his bed at night, or even locked in a cell under the eyes of his jailer, and yet his spirit could roam free as a werewolf."[6]

According to this view, then, a werewolf could mentally attack anyone, anywhere, anytime. This belief made it easy to convict suspected werewolves, even if they were nowhere near the scene of a crime. "Once the charge was made, it was very hard for a person to prove he was not a werewolf,"[7] explains Cohen.

Identifying Werewolves

The task was even harder if a person had certain unfortunate features. Werewolves in human form could be identified, it was once thought, by a long list of physical traits. Any person who possessed these traits was suspected of being a werewolf.

Excessive body hair was one dead giveaway. According to the popular view, people who were werewolves often sported thick, dark hair on their arms, legs, and backs. This hairiness was thought to occur even inside the werewolf's body. Authorities sometimes cut open the skin of accused werewolves to look for their inner fur.

It was easier to spot unusual facial hair, which was said to be another sure sign of lycanthropy. Werewolves usually had eyebrows that met in the middle, as described in this old rhyme:

Beware of him whose eyebrows meet,

For in his heart there lies deceit.[8]

In addition to such brows, werewolves were said to have pointed patches of head hair growing partly down their foreheads. These triangular patches, called widow's peaks, were fairly common. Therefore a widow's peak was not necessarily suspicious on its own. Combined with other clues, however, this type of hair growth could indicate a monstrous nature.

Hairy palms were another wolfish trait. In their human form, true werewolves always had this unusual feature. Hairless palms, however, did not prove that a person was not a werewolf; werewolves

The classic werewolf of myth and legend resembles a real wolf except that it is usually bigger, stronger, faster, smarter, and more cunning than its four-footed canine cousins. It might also have eyes that seem to glow in the dark.

could easily shave their hands. For this reason, werewolf hunters looked not just for palm hair but also for rough skin. They believed that dry, damaged palms could betray frequent shaving.

A person's hands could be revealing in other ways too. The length of the fingers, for instance, could indicate a werewolf nature. The werewolf's ring finger was always longer than the middle finger. Also, the left thumbnail was sometimes long and wickedly pointed. It was thought that the werewolf used this claw to rip its human skin open during the transformation process.

Poor skin condition was one final sign of the werewolf. It was believed that werewolves often got scratched or bruised during their nocturnal romps. These injuries did not disappear when the werewolf returned to its human form; they remained on the skin for anyone to see. People who were always covered with unexplained cuts and welts were, therefore, regarded with suspicion. Neighbors wondered how someone had received these marks—and whether he or she had been in wolf form at the time.

Preventing Werewolf Attacks

Neighbors also wondered how to stay safe if these people were, indeed, werewolves. After all, a person in wolf form was a dangerous thing. If there was any chance that one of these creatures might be roaming nearby, it was only sensible to take protective measures.

It was best, of course, not to encounter the werewolf in the first place. Various werewolf repellents were used to achieve this result. Certain plants, including rye, mistletoe, and mountain ash, were believed to scare away werewolves. Some legends state that a flower called wolfsbane could also do the job. Any of these plants could be carried on the body or hung by the door. If a person was lucky, these simple measures would prevent werewolf attacks.

Magical spells could also offer protection. Travelers commonly recited antiwerewolf poems or phrases before nighttime journeys.

> ## Did You Know?
>
> Under current Argentinian law, seventh sons (who it is said have the potential to be werewolves) can apply to become the godchildren of the president. Most parents are willing to tolerate their "werewolf" children in return for this honor.

For example, a prayer directed to the Roman moon goddess, Diana, reads in part:

> I do beseech thee to drive all werewolves away from my path.
>
> May you change deadly wolf intent and savage heart
>
> back to the human form of gentle man or woman.[9]

Incantations like this one, unfortunately, did not always work. Werewolves sometimes appeared even if a person took every possible precaution. When this happened, stronger measures were required.

Showing silver objects to the creature was one possible choice. This metal was thought to weaken werewolves, much as kryptonite weakens Superman. Any silver item—a knife, a piece of jewelry, even a coin—could do the trick. Werewolves were well aware of this effect, and they wanted nothing to do with it. They were sure to flee at the slightest glimpse of this powerful material.

Flinging clothing at the werewolf was another trick that might work in a pinch. This idea stemmed from the belief that people had to be fully naked before they could transform themselves into wolves. The slightest touch of clothing would undo the spell and force the werewolf back into its human form. The now-human monster might still attack, but a naked man or woman was a lot easier to deal with than a ravening wolf.

Curing Werewolves

Forcing a werewolf into human form was a good strategy for desperate situations. It did not, however, solve the essential problem. The creature might be harmless for the moment, but it was still a werewolf. The dangerous beast would reemerge the moment it got a chance.

To stop this from happening, people tried their best to cure werewolves of their awful affliction. One way they did this was through priestly intervention. It was thought that holy men could sometimes remove the werewolf curse. Werewolves were not especially sensitive to religious influence, though, so this approach was far from a sure thing.

If religion failed, herbs might do the trick. Wolfsbane potions could sometimes strip a werewolf of its powers. This medicine had to be carefully applied, though, because wolfsbane could also induce the werewolf transformation. Handled incorrectly, the treatment could, therefore, make the situation worse instead of better.

Killing Werewolves

The wolfsbane problem was typical of werewolf cures. Most cures were ineffective and could backfire. There was simply no good, proven way to remove the werewolf curse. In fact, the only guaranteed way to stop a werewolf permanently was to kill it.

According to tradition, there were countless ways to accomplish this goal. Werewolves could be shot, stabbed, poisoned, beheaded, or dispatched by any other method. The real danger occurred after death, when the former werewolf might turn into a vampire. A werewolf's remains were always burned to avert this horrifying possibility.

In recent times people seem to have forgotten about the vampire potential. Modern tales do not speak of werewolves rising from the dead. They do, however, show that the process of killing werewolves has gotten much harder over the centuries. Today storytellers claim that the werewolf is nearly immortal, vulnerable to nothing except a silver weapon. Silver bullets are considered especially effective. A wound from a silver-bearing gun is certain to end any werewolf's miserable existence.

It is good that *something* can do the job. Werewolves continue to stalk people's nightmares today, just as they were once thought to stalk actual human victims. Real or not, these creatures are supernaturally scary, and the idea that they can be killed is comforting. It gives people the knowledge—or the illusion, some might say—that they can keep themselves safe when werewolves roam.

Chapter 2

Encounters with Werewolves

Historical records show that many thousands of years ago, holy men called shamans started to assume vital roles in cultures around the world. Shamans tended to the spiritual health of their people. They did this partly by communicating with the animal spirits that were thought to be invisibly present at all times.

The wolf was one of these spirits. A shaman might call upon wolf entities for many types of help: for protection, for luck with the hunt, or for courage. To do so, though, he first had to establish a link with the wolf's essence. He had to feel the wolf, to look through its eyes. In a sense, he had to become the wolf.

In some cultures this process was quite literal. The shaman might don a wolf skin or a tail and pretend to be a wolf. He might also perform wolf-related rituals. If these rituals were successful, it was believed that a wolf spirit would enter the mortal plane and possess the shaman's body. In other words, it would turn the man into a wolf.

Some modern scholars think that the idea of the werewolf originated with this practice. They point out that shamans unquestionably existed, that they tried to summon wolf spirits, and that they sometimes displayed wolf-like traits. It is likely that most of them truly felt they were wolves during these times. The shaman's people, too, felt the wolf's presence. They believed they were witnessing a genuine transformation.

In ancient times, the holy men known as shamans sometimes called upon the spirit of the wolf for protection, luck, and courage. To win the spirit's favor the shaman might have donned a wolf skin or tail and imitated the animal to form a spiritual connection.

Werewolf Warriors

This idea persisted and grew through the ages. People of many times and places have reported encounters with wolf-men. Entire tribes of werewolf warriors even existed in some cultures.

The Laignach Fáelad of ancient Ireland was one such tribe. These fierce soldiers lived in the remote hills of County Tipperary, where they reportedly killed wildlife as well as farmers' herds in a wolf-like fashion. They wore animal pelts and were said to be half man and half wolf. Local residents were terrified of these vicious beings.

The founder of this tribe was mentioned prominently in an Irish text called the *Cóir Anmann*. This work states that "he was the man that used to shift into *fáelad*, i.e. wolf-shapes. He and his offspring after him used to go, whenever they pleased, into the shapes of the wolves, and, after the custom of wolves, kill the herds."[10] Written in the 1500s, this manuscript is one of the few surviving sources to mention Ireland's ancient werewolves.

> **Did You Know?**
>
> In Navajo tradition werewolves are known as skin walkers. Skin walkers are thought to be shamans in wolf form.

Much better documented are the *berserkers* of ancient Scandinavia. The berserkers were Viking warriors who put on shirts made of bearskin or wolf hide before going into battle. These shirts seemed to give the wearers animal attributes. The pelt-clad soldiers were fearless and full of wild rage. They felt no pain, no cold, no hunger—nothing, in fact, but the urge to kill. A fighting berserker seemed so inhuman that it was easy for people to believe that he really was a wolf.

In his classic work on werewolves, Sabine Baring-Gould credits the berserkers with launching the werewolf tradition in Europe. He presents his argument with these words:

The whole superstructure of fable and romance relative to transformation into wild beasts, reposes simply on this basis of truth—that among the Scandinavian nations there existed a form of madness or possession, under the influence of which men acted as though they were changed into wild and savage brutes, howling, foaming at the mouth, ravening for blood and slaughter, ready to commit any act of atrocity, and as irresponsible for their actions as the wolves and bears, in whose skins they often equipped themselves.[11]

Baring-Gould's point is a good one. The berserkers were real, well-documented people who displayed animalistic traits. It would not be much of a stretch for people to imagine this type of change happening in other circumstances.

The Beast of Gévaudan

Most werewolf changes were indeed imaginary. One particular case, though, resists explanation to this day. Historical records show that between 1764 and 1767 a murderous monster roamed the remote French region of Gévaudan. Known as "the Beast of Gévaudan" or simply "La Bête" (which means "the Beast" in French), this werewolf-like creature had an insatiable craving for human flesh. According to modern historians, it is known to have killed at least 113 people. Of these, 98 were partly eaten.

This was the sad case in the Beast's first documented murder, which occurred in July 1764. The creature killed and partly consumed a young girl who was tending a flock of sheep. The girl's family became concerned when the child did not come home that evening, so they went out looking for her. They were horrified to discover her mauled body in a nearby valley.

Other children soon suffered a similar fate. These incidents, not surprisingly, threw the region into a panic—and they also aroused suspicion. No one had ever seen such vicious, consistent animal at-

> **Did You Know?**
>
> Some historians think the Beast of Gévaudan was actually an entire wolf pack. Others have suggested that it might have been a mix between a wolf and a dog or some kind of big cat.

tacks before. People started to think that no normal creature could be responsible. They concluded that they must be dealing with a *loup-garou* (the French word for "werewolf").

Several documented sightings seemed to support this idea. One farmer saw the creature peering into his window and reported that "the werewolf's eyes were glassy, like those of a wild animal, and its dark face was covered with hair."[12] Other witnesses claimed that the Beast was wolf-like but that it walked upright, on its hind legs, and moved like a man in wolf skin. The creature's hide was said to be covered with bristly hair that smelled absolutely awful. People who escaped from the Beast invariably commented on its rank stench.

Comments like these eventually reached the ears of the French king, Louis XV. Appalled, Louis sent out a hunting party that found and slew a large wolf. Yet it was obviously not the culprit because the murders continued.

An engraving from 1764 depicts the capture of the Beast of Gévaudan as it tries to claim its next victim. Witnesses claimed the beast had glassy eyes, a horrible stench, and that it walked upright like a human.

Werewolf Diseases

Certain diseases and disorders give people wolf-like traits. Before these diseases were understood, afflicted people might—just might—have been mistaken for werewolves. The so-called werewolf maladies include the following:

- *Hypertrichosis.* People who suffer from this genetic disorder have completely furry bodies and faces, much like wolves. The gene that causes this condition is even nicknamed the werewolf gene. Hypertrichosis is very rare, but it is very noticeable. It is not hard to see how a person with hypertrichosis might be mistaken for a werewolf.

- *Porphyria.* Also a genetic disorder, this condition causes extreme sensitivity to light along with ugly, raw skin wounds. It can lead to red or "bloody" teeth as well. At one time people who displayed these symptoms were suspected of running about the countryside at night in wolf form.

- *Rabies.* People can catch this disease if they are bitten by a rabid animal. Rabies causes many severe symptoms in humans, including agitation, drooling, convulsions, and a crippling fear of water. Sufferers become mentally unstable and sometimes act like angry wolves, biting and scratching at anyone who comes too close.

The werewolf's reign of terror finally came to an end in 1767 when a local nobleman organized a massive hunt. The hunters soon cornered a wolf-like creature that appeared to be the dreaded Beast, and a man named Jean Chastel shot the animal to death. Some say Chastel used silver bullets made from a blessed chalice to accomplish the deed.

This last part of the story may be an embellishment. The essential tale of the Beast of Gévaudan, though, almost certainly is not. As one author says, "Clearly it was more than just a legend. The records that indicate that something deadly and dangerous was stalking the area in the 1760s are too numerous and too reliable to be ignored."[13] Although no one can say for sure if it was a werewolf, the creature, whatever it might have been, was real—and it left a string of victims behind as proof.

Peter Stubbe

A notorious serial killer named Peter Stubbe also left a trail of death and destruction behind him. Stubbe, who is sometimes referred to as Stumpf, lived in the small German town of Bedburg during the mid-1500s. As a teenager Stubbe realized that his heart was full of evil. He wanted to hurt people, and he begged the devil to help him accomplish this goal. Satan reportedly heard Stubbe's unholy prayer and granted him the power to turn himself into a wolf. As author Montague Summers writes in his classic 1933 book, *The Werewolf,* "The Devil . . . gave unto him a girdle [strap] which, being put around him, he was straight transformed into the likeness of a greedy, devouring wolf, strong and mighty, with great eyes and large, which in the night sparkled like unto brands of fire, a mouth great and wide, with most sharp and cruel teeth, a huge body and mighty paws."[14]

Thrilled with his new abilities, Peter Stubbe embarked on a decades-long killing spree. He preyed mostly on women and children, first murdering and then partly eating them. Stubbe also attacked men who had angered him in some way. He stalked these unlucky victims until they traveled beyond the edge of town. Then he transformed himself into wolf form (or so he later claimed) to strike the fatal blow.

The people of Bedburg knew about these murders, of course. Yet they did not suspect Stubbe of any wrongdoing. He looked and acted like an ordinary citizen in every way. Besides it seemed clear that the attacks were the work of an animal. It was unbelievable that a human could commit such atrocities.

The townspeople were soon to learn, however, that this belief was wrong. In 1589 a group of men and dogs went looking for a missing child that had been carried off by a huge, black, wolf-like creature. The hunting group soon cornered the creature. As the story goes, they were shocked when the beast transformed before their eyes into their neighbor, Peter Stubbe.

Stubbe was taken into custody and questioned. He startled authorities by immediately and proudly confessing that he was a werewolf. Stubbe also confessed to murdering countless people, including his own firstborn son, over the past few decades. All of these crimes, he said, had taken place while he was in wolf form.

This shocking confession left the authorities very little choice. They immediately sentenced Stubbe to death, and the grim sentence was carried out a few days later. There would be no more howling at the moon for history's most notorious werewolf.

Gilles Garnier

The case of Peter Stubbe was unusually clear-cut. His wolfish transformation had been witnessed—or so it was sworn—by dozens of men. The same was not true of Gilles Garnier, an alleged werewolf who terrorized the French town of Dole in 1572. There is little doubt that Garnier committed the crimes of which he was accused. Whether he was in wolf form at the time, however, was never firmly established.

This uncertainty is evident in one classic account of Garnier's misdeeds. Author Sabine Baring-Gould explains that several peasants were walking through the forest one evening when they heard a child screaming and what sounded like a wolf baying. Running to investigate, "they found a little girl defending herself against a

e is heere laide on a Carte wheele nd his flesh pluckt from his bones with hot pincers.   Heere he hath his legges and armes broken vpon a Cart wheele with a woodden Axe.   He hath heer his head strook from his body and stuck vpon a hye pole with the picture of a Woolfe, and 16. peeces of wood, resembling the 16. persons which he had slaine.   Heere is his body with his daughter and gossip burned to ashes. Thus he liued and dyed in the likenes of a woolf, and shape of a man.

monstrous creature, which was attacking her tooth and nail, and had already wounded her severely in five places. As the peasants came up, the creature fled on all fours into the gloom of the thicket; it was so dark that it could not be identified with certainty, and whilst some affirmed that it was a wolf, others thought they had recognized the features of [Garnier]."[15]

Based on this evidence, Garnier was seized and brought to trial. The accused man was a sorry sight on the witness stand. He was

The Werewolf Saint

The biblical figure known as Saint Christopher is a popular character in Roman Catholic and Orthodox Christian traditions. He is known particularly as the protector of travelers. He is also said to guard against many everyday misfortunes, including lightning, disease, floods, and even toothaches.

He might not be much help against werewolves, however; according to Old English legends, he is one! Ancient texts explain that Saint Christopher was originally named Reprobus. Reprobus, it is said, "was one of the Dogheads, a race that had the heads of dogs and ate human flesh."

Another part of this text describes Reprobus's terrifying appearance. The wolf-man, it says, had "a dog's head on him, and long hair, and eyes glittering like the morning star in his head, and his teeth were like the tusks of a wild boar."

Despite his frightening looks, Reprobus had a holy heart. He loved God and performed many services for his Lord, including carrying the Christ child across a raging river. Thanks to this deed and others, Reprobus was appointed a saint after his death and renamed Saint Christopher. Today few Catholics realize that this holy "man" might not have been a man at all.

J. Fraser, "The Passion of St. Christopher," *Revue Celtique*, no. 34, 1913. www.ucc.ie.

stooped and pale, with an unkempt gray beard and bushy eyebrows. He had to be coaxed to speak. When he did, his broadly accented words were barely intelligible. Still, the authorities managed to coax a confession from the unlikely werewolf. Garnier admitted to killing two young girls and a boy. He also said that he had done so in wolf form.

Even at the time, people doubted Garnier's tale. The hermit seemed like a madman, not a monster. Yet Garnier swore that he spoke the truth. As Baring-Gould says, "The poor maniac fully believed that actual transformation into a wolf took place."[16] The townspeople decided that whatever the reality of the situation, Garnier must suffer the usual consequences. He was burned at the stake for lycanthropy, as was customary at the time.

Jean Grenier

Not long after Garnier's execution another self-proclaimed "werewolf" came to trial. The accused was a French teenager named Jean Grenier, who was imprisoned after he attacked a local girl in 1603. Under questioning, Grenier proudly admitted that he was a werewolf. He said he had killed and eaten many children, and he provided dates and locations for these events. It seemed obvious that Grenier really had committed the atrocious acts he described.

But was he a werewolf? Authorities were not sure. They examined the evidence carefully and decided, in the end, that the boy was simply insane. There was no doubt that he was dangerous, but not in any kind of supernatural way: Grenier only *thought* he could turn into a wolf.

In previous times this distinction would not have mattered. Grenier would have been executed as a werewolf anyway. This time, though, the court decided to take a less extreme approach. They sentenced Grenier to life imprisonment in a monastery, where he could be safely contained. The young man spent seven years in these circumstances. As time went by, it became more and more evident that the right decision had been made. Grenier declined steadily over the years, weakening both physically and mentally. He died at age 20 of an unidentified illness that was surely responsible for his werewolf delusions.

The case of Jean Grenier was a milestone in werewolf history. It was the first time a court of law recognized werewolf behavior as a mental disorder rather than an unholy transformation, and this approach marked a lasting change. As Baring-Gould says, "From this time medical men seem to have regarded [lycanthropy] as a form of mental malady to be brought under their treatment, rather than as a crime to be punished by law."[17]

This change meant that fewer supposed werewolves were executed. It did not, however, eliminate these creatures—or the idea of them, anyway. Over the centuries people have continued to believe that they change into wolves under the full moon. Some of these people have undoubtedly hunted and killed during these times. Despite today's medical advances, there will always be people who believe they are werewolves.

Bill Ramsey

The case of a modern-day "werewolf" named Bill Ramsey illustrates this statement. Ramsey was a normal boy until the age of nine, when he felt a peculiar change come over him one day. He remembers the change as a "curious, growing rage that seemed to overtake him like a blinding seizure. Images of himself as a wolf began flashing through his mind. . . . He heard the low, chilling rumble of a frenzied beast and knew that, somehow, it was himself he was hearing."[18]

The fit soon passed, but not for good. Over the next few decades Ramsey experienced similar feelings on several occasions, with the sensation growing stronger each time. People who saw Ramsey during these moments said that he seemed positively wolf-like. "He snarled, howled, foamed at the mouth, curled his lips back and leaped at my men with hands and fingers that looked like the claws of an animal," shuddered a police officer who was called to restrain Ramsey one day. "It was the most frightening thing I've ever seen."[19]

This incident was one of many that occurred during the 1980s. Ramsey's tale began to spread as the so-called Wolfman of London landed repeatedly in jail or in psychiatric units after animalistic rampages. Ramsey became somewhat famous and was even profiled in a major tabloid newspaper. "A Werewolf's Chilling Story—in His

Own Words!"[20] blared the lurid headline that introduced the monstrous write-up.

Thanks to exposure like this, Ramsey's story soon reached the ears of a Roman Catholic bishop. The bishop felt certain that Ramsey was possessed by a demon, and he persuaded the wolf-man to undergo an exorcism. The ritual apparently worked because Ramsey later reported that he had felt an evil spirit leaving his body. The former werewolf was never troubled by animal urges again.

Werewolves Today

No one can say with certainty whether Bill Ramsey was truly possessed or simply suffered from clinical lycanthropy. Whatever the case, it is clear that Ramsey hated his condition. He was desperate to be cured.

Many other modern "werewolves," however, feel very differently. Today there are entire communities of normal, healthy people who claim to have wolf characteristics. These people do not find their wolf sides bothersome in the least. On the contrary, they love the idea of being werewolves. They call themselves "weres" and do everything they can to nurture their animal aspects.

These aspects generally do not include a physical change. Most weres believe that the shift, as they call it, is mental or spiritual. They achieve this change by concentrating on their animal traits. Before long, the inner beast emerges. "What I mean by 'shifted' is the state of mind that I'm in when I feel closest to my animal spirit. . . . It's the state that I envision a healthy animal being in at any given moment . . . ready to fight or flee, ready for anything a hostile world might conjure up,"[21] explains one self-professed were.

The shifting experience is said to be different for everyone. Some people must work hard to achieve it. Others shift involuntarily under the light of the full moon, like classic werewolves. Still others claim that they do, indeed, undergo a physical transformation from human to wolf.

> # Did You Know?
> Some modern-day werewolves call themselves therians, a term that covers all species of human-to-animal shape-shifters.

Most weres scoff at claims like these. They believe that lycanthropy is solely a spiritual state. Some individuals, however, are willing to keep an open mind. "I personally have never seen a man transform physically into an animal, and cannot do it myself; but I'll never rule that possibility out," says one were. "Most people can sense an outward change when I'm shifted inwardly. Perhaps this is the first step, for me, to physical changing."[22]

Tracking Modern Werewolves

This man is not alone in his belief that real werewolves might exist. Many people feel the same way. This fact became evident between 1987 and 1988, when a show called *Werewolf* aired on America's FOX television network. The phone number for a werewolf hotline was given out during this show. The hotline received about 5,000 calls from people who swore they had seen werewolves. It also logged many calls from viewers claiming to be werewolves themselves.

A paranormal investigator named Stephen Kaplan looked into many of these claims. Kaplan, who passed away in 1995, spent several decades of his life studying supernatural creatures. He developed a healthy respect for self-proclaimed werewolves during this time and was always very cautious when he interviewed them. "Many of them have spent time in mental institutions. Many have killed as teenagers and were committed. And the full moon really does affect them,"[23] he said in one interview.

Kaplan admitted that he had never seen a human change fully into a wolf. He had, however, witnessed lesser transformations. "The voice, the posture, the personality changes. In some cases, even eye color changes,"[24] he explained.

Based on these observations and others, Kaplan was convinced that real werewolves did exist. He had a theory that they might be descended from the yeti, which is another term for the abominable snowman. If the yeti crossbred with humans sometime in the distant past, werewolves might be the long-term result.

Could Werewolves Be Real?

This theory, if it is true, might account for some of the werewolf sightings that have been reported in recent decades. In Lawton,

Texas, for example, dozens of people spotted an alleged werewolf in February 1971. The beast was partly dressed in human clothes and it had a human-like body, but it was unusually tall and hairy. It moved like an animal, and it behaved in a wolf-like manner. Witnesses unanimously declared that the creature, whatever it might be, was hideous and horrifying. They were terrified by what seemed to be a genuine werewolf.

In more recent years a creature dubbed "the Bray Road Beast" has turned up in rural Wisconsin. This monster allegedly stalks the town of Delavan and its surroundings. The beast is said to be wolf-like, with glowing yellow eyes and a canine snout. It is tall and hairy, with fangs and pointed ears. Some people say it walks on two legs, like a human. Others say that it travels on all fours, like a wolf. Last sighted in 2005, this monster is widely believed to be a werewolf.

Incidents like these keep the idea of the werewolf alive in modern times. They also pique the interest of various experts, some of whom believe that a werewolf transformation is scientifically possible. "[There is a] powerful link between mind and body," mulls a nuclear physicist in one essay. "It is not such a stretch to argue that, in a few rare instances, a human being could periodically express the physical characteristics of some type of a ferocious animal."[25]

These instances must be rare indeed because they have never occurred under reliable, scientifically documented circumstances. This does not mean, however, that they cannot occur. There is always the chance, no matter how small, that werewolves of the real, physical, man-into-beast variety stalk the world on moonlit nights.

Chapter 3

Werewolves in Literature and Film

Werewolves have been giving people the chills for thousands of years. These monsters prowl through children's nightmares and arouse adults' deepest, most superstitious fears. It seems that humans of every age are repelled—yet somehow fascinated too—by these horrific beasts.

Over the ages these mixed emotions have created a fertile and apparently never-ending source of inspiration for storytellers. Long-ago poets wrote down and embellished the ancient legends of their cultures. In later years novelists in many genres used the werewolf as a character in works of fiction. And today movie screenwriters have given the werewolf a life on the big screen. The result is that werewolf enthusiasts can now enjoy their favorite monster in countless fictional forms.

The Myth of Lycaon

One of the earliest werewolf stories comes from the mythology of ancient Greece. The myth concerns a king named Lycaon who received a visit one day from the god Zeus. Most of Lycaon's people felt honored to receive such a visit, and they treated their guest with great respect. Lycaon, however, thought that Zeus was lying about being a god—and he decided to prove it. He served Zeus a plate of human flesh, fully expecting to fool his guest into cannibalism.

Unfortunately for Lycaon, Zeus was exactly what he claimed to be, so he immediately detected the king's foul trick. The god was furious at the insult, and he took immediate revenge. He called down thunderbolts that destroyed Lycaon's home and killed most of his sons.

The king was horror-struck by this turn of events. He realized he had made a bad mistake, and he also knew that he was in terrible danger. Lycaon fled from Zeus's wrath, but there was no escape for the unlucky king. As Lycaon ran, he lost the ability to speak, and his body took on the shape of a wolf. In a work called *Metamorphoses* from the first century AD, an author named Ovid describes this gruesome moment:

> [Lycaon] ran in terror, and reaching the silent fields howled aloud, frustrated of speech. Foaming at the mouth, and greedy as ever for killing, he turned against the sheep, still delighting in blood. His clothes became bristling hair, his arms became legs. He was a wolf, but kept some vestige of his former shape. There were the same grey hairs, the same violent face, the same glittering eyes, the same savage image.[26]

To the Greek way of thinking, Lycaon's transformation was fearsome but fitting. The king had been a cruel, bloodthirsty human. By turning the tyrant into a wolf, Zeus gave him a form that more closely matched his personality. The myth of Lycaon was, therefore, a moral lesson of sorts. It reminded people that they had better respect their gods because the gods could and would mete out a gruesomely appropriate punishment, if necessary.

Lycaon's story is the best-known ancient werewolf tale. It is not, however, the only one. The werewolf also pops up in the works of Apollodorus, Pliny the Elder, Petronius, and other writers who

Did You Know?

In one version of the story of Lycaon, the king discovers that he likes being a werewolf because it allows him to continue his bloodthirsty ways.

lived and worked around the same time as Ovid. These works and others firmly established the idea of the wolf-man in the public's imagination.

Gothic Horror

In the 1100s a French writer named Marie de France built upon this fascination with a classic tale of love and betrayal. France's narrative poem "Bisclavret" concerns a baron who is secretly a *bisclavret*, or werewolf. The baron's wife and her lover conspire to hide the werewolf's human clothes, thereby forcing him to remain in wolf form. This ruse is eventually uncovered by the local king, who is good friends with the missing baron. The werewolf regains his clothes and his human body. The unfaithful wife is banished from the kingdom along with her lover, never to be seen or heard from again.

"Bisclavret" is a simple tale, based on themes that are very common in werewolf lore. The same cannot be said of George W.M. Reynolds's *Wagner, the Wehr-Wolf*, a work published in England between 1846 and 1847. *Wagner* was a serial novel—or penny dreadful, as these weekly pamphlets were known—and the book was, indeed, plenty dreadful. It focused on an old man named Fernand Wagner who strikes a deal with the devil. The devil will make Wagner young, rich, and smart. In return, Wagner will spend eighteen months as a werewolf.

This decision kicks off a long string of melodrama. The book's 64 installments cover topics ranging from wolfish carnage to doomed love, betrayal, prison breaks, and much more. The tale ends with the death of Wagner, who by now detests his werewolf existence. This is actually a happy ending; Wagner repents of his crimes and earns a spot in heaven as a result.

No such redemption occurs in *The Strange Case of Dr. Jekyll and Mr. Hyde*, a tale written in 1886 by Robert Louis Stevenson. In this well-known story, Dr. Jekyll is a scientist who succeeds in separating

Did You Know?

Suspected werewolf attacks in Gévaudan in eighteenth-century France intrigued author Robert Louis Stevenson, who briefly described the case in one of his early books.

Werewolf Rhyme Time

Werewolf themes have appeared in every imaginable fiction format. These monsters have even inspired some works of poetry. One famous verse appears at the end of a 1921 version of the werewolf-themed fairy tale "Little Red Riding Hood." Written by Charles Perrault, the rhyming moral reads in part:

> Little girls, this seems to say,
> Never stop upon your way.
> Never trust a stranger-friend;
> No one knows how it will end.
> As you're pretty, so be wise;
> Wolves may lurk in every guise.
> Handsome they may be, and kind,
> Gay, or charming never mind!
> Now, as then, 'tis simple truth—
> Sweetest tongue has sharpest tooth!

Perrault's verse is well known among scholars. In terms of popular impact, though, no werewolf poem can match a ditty from the 1941 film *The Wolf Man*. First spoken in the movie by a gypsy woman, the verse describes the human-to-wolf connection:

> Even the man who is pure in heart
> And says his prayers by night,
> May become a wolf when the wolfsbane blooms
> And the autumn moon is bright.

This verse is repeated several times during the film. Viewers remembered it long after they left the theater—and they are still remembering it today. Simple and catchy, this rhyming phrase is probably the most famous quotation in any work of werewolf fiction.

Charles Perrault, *Old Time Stories Told by Master Charles Perrault*, trans. Alfred Edwin Johnson. New York: Dodd, Mead, 1921. www.angelfire.com.

The Wolf Man. DVD. Directed by George Waggner, 1941; Universal Pictures, August 30, 2009.

the good and evil sides of his personality. He undergoes a physical change when he switches from one aspect to the other. Although Stevenson never explains exactly what this shift entails, he seems to be hinting that the scientist is a werewolf.

In one passage Stevenson teases readers by letting them see the beginning of Jekyll's remarkable transformation. Just before the moment of change, Jekyll is sitting at his window, chatting pleasantly with two colleagues below. Then, out of the blue, "the smile was struck out of his face and succeeded by an expression of such abject terror and despair, as froze the very blood of the two gentlemen below. They saw it but for a glimpse for the window was instantly thrust down."[27] Readers are left to decide for themselves what happened behind that closed window. Some kind of change was obviously taking place. It is entirely possible that the change turned Jekyll from a man into a ravening wolf.

A New Approach

Stevenson may have been cautious about his readers' delicate sensibilities. Later authors, however, were not so inclined to leave things to the imagination. As the decades passed, works of fiction began to describe werewolves and their actions in every monstrous detail.

Guy Endore's *The Werewolf of Paris* was one of the first works to tackle this task. Published in 1933, this novel concerns a young man named Bertrand who was born a werewolf. Bertrand commits countless murders in his wolf state, and Endore mercilessly chronicles every aspect of the slaughter. In this respect Endore's work broke new ground in the field of werewolf literature.

The novel was innovative in other ways as well. It was especially unusual in the way it took the werewolf's viewpoint during his animal changes. One early passage, for example, describes the feelings that overcome Bertrand when he sees a man walking alone down a dark country lane:

A wild desire to lay his hands on that man coursed through Bertrand's body and set his brain aflame. His eyes were so hot that he could not blink without a stab of pain. Every part of his body was sore and so sensitive that every stitch of clothing on his back pressed on his skin like the point of a needle. He quickly disengaged himself therefrom, tearing the buttons off in his haste.[28]

Later in the book Bertrand is terrified when he actually feels himself developing a wolf's physical features: "He panted through his opened mouth. And he felt his tongue, his tongue, the short and bulky tongue of man, begin to flatten and lengthen. 'God help me!' he cried. But now that tongue was curling out of his mouth, was hanging over his teeth."[29]

Descriptions like these might not seem shocking to modern audiences. In the early 1900s, though, they were creative, chilling—and commercially successful. Readers clearly enjoyed stepping outside the lines of conventional werewolf fiction.

Into the Modern Age

Other writers took notice of this reaction. Over subsequent decades they followed Endore's lead by bringing their own twists to the werewolf genre. In his 1940 novel, *Darker than You Think*, for example, author Jack Williamson delved into the science behind lycanthropy and other forms of shape-shifting. Likewise, in *The Howling* (1977), author Gary Brandner introduced an entire town of werewolves. The main character finds herself fighting off a legion of creatures that are neighbors by day, monsters by night.

Books like these increased readers' interest in werewolves. It was not until 1983, though, that the werewolf got the ultimate stamp of literary approval: the attention of famed horror author Stephen King. King gave wolf-men his distinctive treatment in *Cycle of the Werewolf*, a novella that featured illustrations by fantasy artist Bernie Wrightson. The work was embraced enthusiastically by King's already-enormous audience, and this exposure catapulted werewolves to a whole new level of fame.

The publishing world has never looked back. Today werewolf fiction is more monstrously popular than ever before. Werewolf-themed series, in particular, feed fans' appetites for all things wolf. Multiple-book offerings such as Kelley Armstrong's *Bitten*, Stephen Cole's *The Wereling*, and Patricia Brigg's *Moon Called* series hold spots on every werewolf lover's must-read list.

Werewolves in Young-Adult Literature

Traditional werewolf literature can be a bit too intense for underage audiences. In recent years, however, two immensely popular offerings have made werewolves accessible to a younger crowd. J.K. Rowling's *Harry Potter* series includes a werewolf professor, and Stephenie Meyers's *Twilight* series features a whole tribe of wolf-men. More human than monstrous, these characters have captured the hearts of young adults everywhere.

Rowling's werewolf character, Professor Remus Lupin, captures a young Harry Potter's heart as well. Lupin first appears in *Harry Potter and the Prisoner of Azkaban*, the third book in the Harry Potter series. The Hogwarts teacher soon becomes a father figure to Harry, who lost his parents as a young child. Lupin is portrayed as a gentle person who struggles to hide his werewolf nature from Harry and the other students.

This struggle makes for some very interesting reading. As one critic says, "Lupin doesn't see [his werewolf nature] as a plus of course, but it's a very cool extra component to the character, as we see this thoughtful, warm man work to control the monster he turns into."[30] Likable yet tortured, Remus Lupin is a fascinating entry into the werewolf canon.

The same is true of the *Twilight* werewolves. The wolf-men in this series are descended from a long line of shape-shifters who are the sworn enemies of vampires. This fact creates endless problems for Bella Swan, the main female character, who loves the vampire Edward Cullen while being a good friend of the werewolf Jacob Black. Edward and Jacob tolerate each other for Bella's sake—but just barely. Jacob and his kin cannot always stop themselves from shifting into wolf shape, reflexively, when they see Edward or others of his kind.

Written descriptions of this change are exciting. To modern readers, though, they are not always satisfying. People want to see Jacob, Remus Lupin, and other characters shift into wolf form before their very eyes—and today, these people have gotten their wish. The entire *Harry Potter* franchise now appears on film in eight big-budget movies. The *Twilight* series, too, has made the leap to the big screen. Immensely popular, these films give people another way to appreciate their favorite werewolf characters.

Early Werewolf Films

Werewolves have been a popular subject for horror filmmakers since 1913, when the first werewolf-themed movie was released. Entitled simply *The Werewolf*, this silent film starred Phyllis Gordon as a Navajo wolf-woman named Watuma. Watuma assumes wolf shape to fight invading white men after her husband's untimely death. Filmmakers used a real wolf to portray Watuma in her animal form.

No such explicit change occurs in *Wolf Blood* (1925), another silent feature that was more a psychological drama than a horror flick. This film concerns a logging company foreman who receives an emergency transfusion of wolf blood. Afterward the foreman believes he is a werewolf. No transformation occurs on-screen, but there are plenty of wolf dreams and wolf-related murders. Usually

In the Twilight *series of books and movies, werewolves are the sworn enemies of vampires. But two of the central characters, Edward Cullen the vampire (left) and Jacob Black the werewolf (right), tolerate each other for the sake of the story's human heroine, Bella Swan (center).*

the twilight saga
eclipse

IT ALL BEGINS...WITH A CHOICE.

cited as the first full-length werewolf film, this movie was a milestone of its genre.

The first true werewolf hit, though, was yet to come. In 1935 Universal Pictures released a full-color, full-sound production entitled *The Werewolf of London*. Starring Henry Hull in the title role, this film concerns a scientist named Wilfred Glendon who is bitten by a werewolf while journeying in Tibet. Glendon soon starts to turn into a werewolf. The scientist struggles against the forces that now possess him, but he is driven to increasing acts of violence. A silver bullet eventually cures the man of his hated condition.

The Werewolf of London is notable partly because it was history's first major-studio werewolf production. It is also remembered for its creative approach to the werewolf change. The initial transformation, for example, occurs as Glendon walks behind a series of pillars. Each time the scientist appears in a gap, he looks more like a wolf. It was a smart solution that one critic describes as "a memorable, wonderfully artistic little sequence which deserves to have 'classic horror scene' status."[31]

Later scenes were equally innovative. In one scene the camera pans back and forth between Glendon's hands and his face. With each shot, the actor gets a little bit hairier. The transformation is totally believable, which was quite an accomplishment considering the modest resources of the era. "It's impressive, bearing in mind that this was really the first time they'd tried to achieve this, and they had very few references to fall back on,"[32] enthuses one film writer.

Big Studios, Big Monsters

As good as it was, *The Werewolf of London* was just a warm-up. Universal Pictures was getting ready to release a film that was destined to become the must-see werewolf classic of all time. Called *The Wolf Man*, this 1941 picture starred Lon Chaney Jr. as an unfortunate man named Larry Talbot. Talbot is bitten by a werewolf during a trip to his native Wales and soon begins to develop were-

Keeping Monstrous Company

Werewolves and vampires are entirely different creatures. In recent years, however, these monsters have become a package deal in some writers' minds. The *Twilight* series is a standout example of this trend, but it is far from the only one. Today many prominent books and films explore the imaginary relationship between wolf-men and the undead.

This is the case in the popular *Underworld* film series. Launched in 2003, this franchise concerns a universe where vampires and lycans (human-wolf shape-shifters) are sworn enemies. These creatures live incognito among humans and must conduct their countless bloody battles in utmost secrecy.

The enemy theme was also central to the 2004 blockbuster *Van Helsing*. In this film, Dracula is terrorizing the world, and only a werewolf can stop him. At one point the fiends engage in an epic struggle unlike anything seen before in the werewolf or vampire genre.

Vampire/werewolf battles also occur from time to time in Charlaine Harris's *Southern Vampire Mysteries* series, which is the basis for HBO's smash hit *True Blood*. In Harris's fictional world, magical creatures of many types live openly among humans. Vampires and werewolves dislike each other and sometimes fight viciously. They can get along, though, if they are trying to reach a common goal.

wolf traits himself. Murder, mayhem, and the inevitable werewolf hunt follow.

There was nothing terribly original about *The Wolf Man*'s story line, but audiences loved the movie anyway. Modern film critics credit much of this positive response to Chaney's unique look. In the hands of master Universal makeup artist Jack Pierce, Chaney morphed into an explosively hairy beast with sharp teeth, claw-like fingernails, and disturbingly human eyes. It reportedly took five hours each morning to create this look and another two hours to remove it when the day's filming was done. Chaney said later that the process was sheer torture.

The result, however, turned out to be worth the effort. Chaney's character captured the public's imagination and, in time, came to define the werewolf for many moviegoers. As one critic says, "For millions of contemporary men and women, the very word 'werewolf' conjures up images of the actor Lon Chaney, Jr."[33]

This might be partly due to the fact that Chaney did not stop with one werewolf project. *The Wolf Man* was so popular that it spawned four sequels. Chaney repeated his role as Larry Talbot in *Frankenstein Meets the Wolf Man* (1943), *House of Frankenstein* (1944), *House of Dracula* (1945), and *Abbott and Costello Meet Frankenstein* (1948), all from Universal Pictures. By the time this run ended, Universal's version of the werewolf was firmly embedded in the public mind.

This success did not deter rival Hammer Studios from making its own werewolf movie shortly thereafter. *The Curse of the Werewolf*, which was released in 1961, was loosely based on Guy Endore's novel *The Werewolf of Paris*. It featured a fine performance by Oliver Reed as the title creature. "[Reed] gives a moving and chilling portrayal of the stricken young man . . . and the make-up job for the creature is good enough that it stands the test of time,"[34] reports one modern viewer. Now considered a classic, this well-received film was Hammer's only foray into the werewolf genre.

Building on a Theme

Other studios, however, would soon pick up the slack. Encouraged by the success of Universal and Hammer, various moviemakers started

to toy with the werewolf theme. They tried many new approaches to this old subject.

One standout offering was called *An American Werewolf in London.* Released in 1981, this film focuses on two young American men who take a backpacking holiday in England. One of the friends dies in a moonlight werewolf attack. The other friend, David, is mauled, but he survives—much to his eventual distress. Throughout the rest of the film, David copes with confusing and painful changes as he turns little by little into a werewolf.

David's first change is a standout moment in movie makeup history. The scene lasts for two and a half agonizing minutes and lets viewers share every painful moment of David's transformation. First the man's hands and feet lengthen. Then his body sprouts hair and starts to twist and distort itself until David can no longer stand upright. Now on all fours, the man's face stretches into a wolf-like mask. His screams of pain become howls as the werewolf change draws to a merciful close.

This scene earned *An American Werewolf in London* the 1981 Academy Award for Outstanding Achievement in Makeup. It is so realistic that it is hard to watch even today, and it was considered even more shocking in its original time. There is no question that it disturbed viewers, but it also delighted them—and it left them hungry for all things werewolf.

Filmmakers happily fed this appetite with two other major-studio 1981 releases. One of these films, *The Howling*, was based on Gary Brandner's 1977 novel of the same name. This movie was so popular that it eventually spawned seven sequels. The second film, *Wolfen*, is a straight-up horror fest about a band of shape-shifting wolf-men who terrorize New York City. Scary and gory, both of these films targeted hard-core horror fans.

Four years later a movie called *Teen Wolf* took an entirely different approach. This goofy 1985 comedy features Michael J. Fox as Scott Howard, a teen who inherits his family's werewolf curse. The boy soon discovers that "the Wolf," as he calls his animal form, is much cooler than plain old Scott. He, therefore, starts spending most of his time in wolf shape. Mostly a reflection on the high-school social scene, this film promotes an ancient hound to top-dog status.

A Modern Monster

Today the werewolf still holds this spot in the movie world, thanks to many big-budget releases that have kept the beast's legacy alive. Some films have attracted attention with big-name actors. The 1994 release *Wolf*, for example, starred the incomparable Jack Nicholson as a man-turned-werewolf and Michelle Pfeiffer as his love interest. More recently, *Red Riding Hood* (2011) used the talents of Amanda Seyfried, Lukas Haas, and horror veteran Gary Oldman to bring a new twist to a classic fairy tale. In this film Red Riding Hood discovers more than she bargained for about a loved one's secret were-wolf identity—and her own dark potential—when she makes her famous trip to Grandma's house.

Other werewolf films have combined movie genres and there-by expanded their potential audiences. The 2002 film *Dog Soldiers*, for example, concerns a routine military exercise that goes awry when soldiers encounter a band of werewolves. The ensuing battle draws upon the conventions of both military and horror films—and succeeds in capturing both. Action-packed and scary, this across-the-boards fan favorite is now considered a modern classic.

To the die-hard werewolf fan, of course, there is no such thing as a "modern classic." Only the true classics matter. Movie studios have tried to please these people by reworking decades-old werewolf offerings. The 2010 film *The Wolfman*, for example, was a big-budget remake of the 1941 classic. *An American Werewolf in London*, too, is scheduled for a facelift; a major studio has taken steps toward remaking the movie. This prospect fills some horror fans with, well, horror. "No, no, no, no, this is all wrong. . . . There isn't any part of this movie in my mind that would benefit from a remake,"[35] wails one unhappy viewer on an Internet message board.

Other fans, while skeptical, are taking a wait-and-see approach. "Remakes are the same as fresher movies—they range from terrible to pretty [darn] good. I say go for it,"[36] writes one werewolf enthusiast. This person will undoubtedly get his wish. Movie studios are desperate to find new, fresh "meat" for werewolf fans everywhere. Remakes and original films will attempt to fill this need in years to come. Written werewolf fiction will do the same thing. As long as people love werewolves, storytellers in all formats will keep this monstrous legend alive.

Chapter 4

Werewolves in Popular Culture

In long-ago times people in many areas considered werewolves to be a real and present danger. They worried about these creatures constantly. They also took steps to identify and avoid them. Through unflagging vigilance, they hoped to keep the werewolf at bay.

This watchful attitude has faded in modern times. Few people nowadays expect to encounter werewolves during a moonlit stroll. This lack of belief, however, does not mean that people have lost interest in humankind's shape-shifting enemy. On the contrary, the public fascination with werewolves is stronger than ever—and this fascination is reflected in countless formats. From television to music, games to sports, and much more, the werewolf is a staple in practically every area of modern popular culture.

A Television Staple

Television is one of these areas. Werewolves have been stalking the small screen since the earliest days of black-and-white television. The story lines behind these appearances often have little or nothing to do with traditional werewolf lore, but this does not seem to bother audiences. Wolf-men are so recognizable that no explanation is needed when they show up.

This was definitely the case on *The Munsters*, a popular sitcom that featured a puzzling yet pleasing monster family. The family's mother and grandfather were vampires; the father was a Frankenstein-like creature; and young Eddie, the family's only child, was a werewolf cub. Eddie looked mostly human, but he had a pronounced widow's peak, bushy eyebrows, pointed ears, and fangs. He revealed his wolf nature by occasionally howling at the moon. He also had a treasured doll called Woof Woof that looked just like Lon Chaney Jr.'s character from *The Wolf Man*. Eddie adored the doll and treated it like the little wolfish brother it appeared to be.

The Munsters aired on CBS from 1964 to 1966, amassing 70 episodes during its run. The show was hugely popular and so was

The Munsters, *a zany 1960s television series about a family of monsters, included a werewolf cub named Eddie, pictured with the rest of the family in this portrait. Eddie looked and acted like other little boys, except for certain facial features and his occasional howling at the moon.*

its wolf-boy, who is now something of a cult figure. Little Eddie has been spoofed on many modern shows, including *Saturday Night Live*, *The Simpsons*, *The Ben Stiller Show*, and others. The fact that audiences still recognize this decades-old character is a testament to the werewolf's inhuman staying power.

Eddie Munster is probably the most famous television werewolf, yet he is far from the only one. Werewolves have played important roles on many popular shows, including the hits *Monster Force*, *Buffy the Vampire Slayer*, and *Charmed*. In more recent years a werewolf character even became a regular on the Disney Channel's *Wizards of Waverly Place*. In the show's third and fourth seasons, teenage wizard Alex dates a werewolf named Mason Greybeck. The young couple must deal with various issues caused by Mason's lycanthropic nature.

The roles of Mason Greybeck, Eddie Munster, and other recurring werewolf characters are substantial. They give viewers something to sink their teeth into. The werewolf does not have to be the star of the show, however, to catch people's attention. Werewolves have had single-episode or bit parts in countless shows, from *Scooby Doo* and *Doctor Who* to *The X-Files* and *CSI: Crime Scene Investigation*. No matter how small their role, these monsters always add a little bite to the productions in which they appear.

> ## Did You Know?
> Film director Quentin Tarantino loves Fruit Brute cereal. He has featured this werewolf-themed food in his movies *Reservoir Dogs* and *Pulp Fiction*.

Monstrous Sales Skills

In the television world, werewolves are not just good characters. They apparently have fantastic advertising skills, too, because werewolves have appeared in many major television commercials over the years. Companies seem to hope that the werewolf's monstrous appeal will make food, medicines, and other everyday objects irresistible to the buying public.

The most successful "spokeswolf" of all time was probably the cartoon creature that hawked General Mills' Fruit Brute cereal. Sold

Stalking the Small Screen

When werewolves show up on television, they usually have bit parts. A few series, though, have put these mythical creatures in the spotlight. These three shows in particular are considered essential viewing by werewolf lovers.

- *Werewolf* (1987–1988). This FOX horror series followed the adventures of Eric Cord, a college student who becomes a werewolf. Hoping to get rid of his curse, Cord embarks on a quest to find and kill the originator of his werewolf bloodline.

- *Being Human* (2008–). Originally broadcast on the British channel BBC Three and remade for North American audiences by the Syfy channel, this show concerns a werewolf, a vampire, and a ghost who share an apartment. The monstrous roommates try their best to live normal lives and blend in with the humans around them.

- *Teen Wolf* (2011–). Launched on MTV in mid-2011, this show was an instant hit. Like the movie that inspired it, *Teen Wolf* is about a high-school student trying to juggle his werewolf identity with his human life and friends. The television series is much darker in tone, however, than the 1985 comedy.

from 1975 to 1983, Fruit Brute contained frosted fruit-flavored flakes and lime-flavored marshmallows. Television commercials for the sugary breakfast treat showed a werewolf howling "FRUUUUUIT!" under a full moon. "With the howling good taste of fruit!"[37] enthused each commercial's final line.

The Sonic Burgers chain has also used a werewolf to sell food. In a 2011 commercial a man and his werewolf buddy sit in the front seat of a car, preparing to eat Sonic's Blazin' BBQ Loaded Burger. The werewolf is nervous about taking a bite—and it turns out that his fear is well founded. The burger is so spicy that the werewolf's fur catches on fire, leaving the creature singed and smoking. "That's got a nice burn,"[38] the monster exclaims as his friend giggles.

Based on this commercial, it is easy to imagine that Sonic's red-hot treat might leave a person—or a werewolf, for that matter—with a serious case of indigestion. If this happens, another werewolf-related product might come to the rescue. In 1991 a Mexican ad for the popular antacid Alka-Seltzer featured a businessman who turned into a wolf due to a terrible stomachache. Two Alka-Seltzer tablets cured the man instantly and allowed him to return to a high-powered meeting.

A television critic commented amusingly on this ad in a 2011 write-up. "Alka-Seltzer, as everyone knows, is a leading remedy for various upset stomach issues. It is also apparently an effective agent against sudden bouts of lycanthropy. . . . [This commercial] proves incontrovertibly that you should come packing Alka-Seltzer tablets alongside your silver bullets for any werewolf fight,"[39] he says.

This admittedly tongue-in-cheek summary does not, of course, capture the point of the Alka-Seltzer ad. The point is to sell a product, and in that respect, the ad clearly succeeded. People are still talking about the commercial decades after it aired. This type of buzz occurs only once in a blue moon—or perhaps, in this case, once in a full moon. The werewolf touch transformed this simple message into advertising gold.

The Music of the Night

Werewolves have shown the same golden touch in the world of music. Over the decades many popular songs have included werewolf references.

Warren Zevon's "Werewolves of London" leads the pack in this genre. First released in 1978, this song's lyrics describe a werewolf who eats Chinese food, hangs out at Trader Vic's, and has perfect hair and clothes. A catchy piano-based tune and a simple chorus of "Ah-OOOO! Werewolves of London!"[40] make this song easy to remember and easy to love. Rising to number 21 on the American Top 40 charts in mid-1978, this tune was the biggest hit of Zevon's career.

Musician Waddy Wachtel, who cowrote the song, is still amazed by this success. During a 2008 interview, Wachtel recalled his shock when "Werewolves of London" was released as a single. He and Zevon both thought the track was weak compared to others on the same album: "Warren and I were completely insulted! 'What's wrong with these people?!' And sure enough, it became the biggest hit Warren ever had."[41]

Perhaps Wachtel should not have been so surprised. Less than a decade earlier the band Creedence Clearwater Revival had scored a huge hit with its 1969 song "Bad Moon Rising." This tune reached number two on American charts in May 1969 and number one in the United Kingdom that September, and it is still popular on classic rock radio stations today. It is often cited as the biggest werewolf-themed song of all time.

A look at the track's lyrics, however, reveals a surprising fact: The song actually has nothing to do with monsters of any type. It concerns an approaching apocalypse of hurricanes, lightning, and floods. Nonetheless, people cannot help thinking of werewolves when they hear the song's refrain:

Don't go around tonight

Well it's bound to take your life

There's a bad moon on the rise.[42]

These evocative words have earned "Bad Moon Rising" a spot on several werewolf-movie soundtracks. Thanks to this usage, the tune has established an unshakeable reputation as a werewolf song. It is forever linked in people's minds with the full moon and the deadly beasts that roam beneath it.

Werewolves in Music Videos

"Bad Moon Rising" is not the only song to make this leap. In recent decades many musical acts have chosen to bring werewolf themes into their otherwise werewolf-free work. They do this mostly through music videos, which allow artists to create movie-like story lines for their songs.

The first notable video to take this approach is still considered one of the best. Michael Jackson's video for the 1983 song "Thriller" is a 14-minute epic that features a horde of dancing zombies and ghouls. In one memorable scene Jackson is walking down a dark lane with his girlfriend when the full moon appears. Jackson immediately begins to writhe in agony. He soon turns into a horrible creature that is meant to be a were-cat; however, many viewers interpret the beast as a werewolf. Jackson's terrified girlfriend flees as the creature bares its fangs and prepares to attack.

The transformation sequence in this video is eerily similar to the one that occurs in *An American Werewolf in London*. This similarity is no accident. Michael Jackson knew about the film and hired its director, John Landis, to help develop the "Thriller" video. During a 2009 interview, Landis remembered Jackson's initial call. "I want to turn into a monster. Can I do that?" Jackson asked. In response, Landis recalled, "I went to see him [and] took along a big book of monsters for him to look at."[43] Jackson identified the look he wanted, and a new chapter in werewolf history was written.

Other artists added their own chapters in later years. The Backstreet Boys, for instance, paid homage to "Thriller" with their 1997 video for the song "Everybody (Backstreet's Back)." In this clip the Boys must sleep in a haunted house after their tour bus breaks down. They dream about being movie monsters during the frightful night that follows. One band member becomes a werewolf that dances, sings, and even does back flips across a deserted ballroom.

The rock band Evanescence has also turned to werewolves for inspiration. The 2006 video for the song "Call Me When You're Sober" features lead singer Amy Lee dressed as Little Red Riding Hood, petting a pack of wolves. Lee's boyfriend in the video has

Wolfman Jack

Werewolves are bloodthirsty, vicious . . . and totally cool, man! This was the message broadcast nightly by Wolfman Jack, one of the most famous disc jockeys (DJs) in radio history. With his signature gravelly speech, the Wolfman rose to fame as the voice of rock and roll in the 1960s and 1970s.

Wolfman Jack did not claim to be a werewolf. He looked a bit like one, though, thanks to his bushy hair, heavy eyebrows, and pointed goatee. The DJ also brought many wolf elements into his work. He regularly howled on air, for instance, and he made references to the full moon. The act was unusual, but it worked. Audiences loved the Wolfman's shtick and tuned in every night to get their werewolf on.

Some people feel that Wolfman Jack's mystique waned a bit in the 1970s, when the DJ started to make frequent public appearances. "Somehow it was a disappointment to see the man in the flesh," remembers one fan. "I wanted to carry on believing that he was a kind of half-human, half-animal creature."

He was not, of course. Wolfman Jack was all too human and he proved it in 1995, when he died unexpectedly of a massive heart attack. Fans everywhere mourned that a beloved icon would howl no more.

Quoted in Sarah Cuddon, "What Made Wolfman Jack Great?," BBC News, March 21, 2008. http://newsvote.bbc.co.uk.

shaggy, beast-like hair and odd eyes. He looks like he could morph into a werewolf at any second. He never actually does it, but this does not detract from the video's impact. The werewolf message—and the feeling of implied danger it carries—comes through loud and clear.

A Comical Beast

There is nothing subtle or implied about comic books, another format that sometimes features werewolves. Graphic artists are limited only by their own creativity. This means that they can make their monsters as outrageous as they like—and they can bring readers along for the ride. Following this approach, several werewolf-related comics have risen to popular success.

A Marvel Comics series called *Werewolf by Night* is part of this group. The first volume of this series ran for 43 issues between 1972 and 1977. Its story line concerns a young man named Jack Russell who inherits his family's werewolf curse on his eighteenth birthday. Russell must learn how to deal with this uncomfortable reality. At the same time, he must fight off a legion of monstrous enemies who seek to use his newfound powers to their advantage.

Uneven story lines and substandard art eventually spelled doom for *Werewolf by Night*. The character of Jack Russell, however, is far from dead. He has made appearances in many other Marvel titles, popping up as recently as 2009. His most notable resurrection occurred in 1998, when Marvel decided to publish *Werewolf by Night: Volume 2*. This offering featured grittier art and story lines than the original series, but it was not embraced by fans. The series lasted just six issues before getting the silver bullet from company executives.

Also lasting just a few issues was Moonstone's *Werewolf: The Apocalypse* line of comics. Released between 2001 and 2003, these five publications were never meant to be a cohesive series. They told stand-alone stories about the werewolf characters from a popular role-playing game of the same name. With their lavish illustrations and interesting story lines, these comics found a niche among apocalypse enthusiasts.

Role-Playing Games

These comics, however, were not as beloved as the role-playing game itself. The board game Werewolf: The Apocalypse was part of White Wolf Gaming Studio's Old World of Darkness line from 1991 to

2004. This line included many role-playing games that shared one imaginary universe. The werewolf version is described as "a game of savage horror in which the Garou [werewolves] . . . fight against the forces of spiritual corruption in hopes of saving Gaia, the Earth herself."[44] Players follow the conceptual guidelines of this story to develop unique werewolf characters. These characters then interact with others to create original situations and story lines.

Werewolf: The Apocalypse and other games in the Old World of Darkness line were very popular. They were so popular, in fact, that they eventually spawned a whole new universe. White Wolf's New World of Darkness line was introduced in 2005 as a replacement for the old line, which is now retired. The New World of Darkness includes a game called Werewolf: The Forsaken that is more personal in tone than the previous version. Featuring all-new settings and rules, this game gives players a new way to tell the werewolf story.

Other role-playing games, while not as popular as White Wolf's offerings, have done the same thing. In the 1991 game NightLife, for example, players chose to be one of seven different night-roaming monsters. The werewolf was one of these choices. These creatures and their relative races lived secretly among humans, performing various tasks to earn strength and life-experience points.

In modern times a similar game exists online. Players of RedMoon Studios' *MonsterGames* choose to be either vampires or werewolves. They seek victims online by posting links to their character's home page. If someone clicks unsuspectingly on one of these links, the player earns game points, food, and other monstrous goodies. This creative yet simple approach breathes new life into an old format and helps to keep the werewolf legend alive.

> **Did You Know?**
>
> The comic character Captain America was a werewolf at one point. He became a lycanthrope named "Cap Wolf" in several 1992 issues.

Werewolves in Video Games

The role-playing format is not for everyone. Some people prefer less thinking and more, more, more action. Werewolf-themed video games may appeal to this crowd. There are several choices in this genre, all of which have earned strong fan bases over the years.

The 1992 game *Wolfchild* is fondly remembered by many gamers. Originally released for the Atari and Amiga systems, *Wolfchild* lets players manipulate a character named Saul across a series of platforms and levels. Saul is human at first, but he turns into a werewolf if a player earns enough energy. Werewolf Saul has superhuman abilities that help him to overcome various enemies and obstacles.

The Beast Within: A Gabriel Knight Mystery is another classic fan favorite. Released in 1995, this PC/Macintosh game was among the first to use full-motion video clips. Players help characters Gabriel Knight and Grace Nakimura to investigate a series of murders in Germany. The murders are vicious, like the work of an animal—or could it be a werewolf? The mystery unfolds scene by horrifying scene as players work their way through the puzzle. "It's an excellent and very scary game. Turn off all the lights and play it in the dark, if you dare!"[45] enthused one player in a 2000 review.

Reviewers were less thrilled with *Altered Beast*, a 2005 PlayStation 2 game sold briefly in Europe and Japan. This game features a main character named Luke Custer who has several microchips in his brain. Each chip contains the genetic code for a different animal. Custer can change into these animals—including, of course, a wolf—whenever the need arises. Known in the gaming community as a "beat 'em up," this game never really caught on due to a weak story line and some annoying game-play flaws.

Tough Stuff

One of these flaws involved the werewolf itself. This character, complained players, was actually a little too good. The beast's speed, strength, and other preternatural powers made the game too easy. These qualities might be considered negatives in the video-game realm. In the real world, however, they can be huge assets. Many organizations and people want to be speedy, strong, and fierce—or to seem that way at least. They sometimes use werewolf ideas and images to communicate this tough-guy image.

A couple of sports teams have taken this approach. The Werewolves of London, for example, have been playing ice hockey in an English league since 2002. This special-needs youth team uses a cartoonish wolf head on its gear. There is also a Polish American Football

League team called the Werewolves that has a snarling man-wolf as its logo. Based in Warsaw, Poland, this team's cheerleading squad is called the She-Wolves.

Sports teams are not the only organizations that hope to intimidate opponents. Military units have the same goal, so it is not surprising that werewolf imagery has shown up in this area as well. In the United States, for instance, the Marine Corps' Marine Fighter Attack Squadron 122 goes by the nickname "the Werewolves." The image of a snarling, clawing wolf graces the squadron's uniforms and equipment.

This type of use makes a modest impact. For sheer in-your-face bravado, though, little can match a semiprofessional wrestler who goes by the name "El Chupacabra, the Mexican Werewolf." "Chupy," as this character is sometimes called, wears wicked false fangs and slitted yellow contact lenses. His shaggy hair gives him an unkempt, ready-to-rumble look. Known for his beastly behavior in the ring, this fighter has amassed a pack of dedicated fans.

In a promotional spot, the animalistic athlete gives these fans a taste of his werewolf wrath. "I am so ready just to sink my teeth into the competition, get that nice warm-blooded taste into my mouth, and spit it right back into your face. . . . If you think you can go toe to toe with the Mexican Werewolf, then you know what? Bring it!!"[46] snarls this werewolf wannabe.

El Chupacabra's presentation is unusual, to say the least. Some people might consider it a bit over the top, but wrestling fans seem to love the entire performance. They appreciate the wrestler's campy confidence as well as his werewolf persona. In the ring or out, the Mexican Werewolf gives people one more way to enjoy their favorite monster.

In Love with Werewolves

Today werewolf enthusiasts can find thousands of werewolf-related products on the market. These products give people countless opportunities to flaunt their love for all things wolf. T-shirts, for instance, proudly declare "I ♥ Werewolves!" or perhaps "Team Jacob," in a reference to *Twilight*'s popular shape-shifting character. Trendy jewelry incorporates werewolf claws, fangs, and other artifacts. Pins, posters, and even bumper stickers communicate a werewolf message to the world at large.

Around Halloween there are even more ways to display one's inner wolf. Costume stores carry werewolf masks, claws, fangs, ears, and other accessories that let regular folks transform themselves into wolfish creatures. The options range from cute and cuddly to vicious and bloody. By picking and choosing among these options, would-be werewolves can create looks that perfectly reflect the monsters they would like to be. People who dress as werewolves are, in a sense, putting their "inner animals" on display. By doing so, they remind the world that every person has a little bit of beast hiding within—and that is the reason behind the werewolf's enduring popularity. Today, as in ages past, people are frightened yet fascinated by the monster they sense within themselves.

Source Notes

Introduction: From Man to Beast

1. George W.M. Reynolds, *Wagner, the Wehr-Wolf,* chap. 12. Project Gutenberg. www.gutenberg.org.

Chapter One: What Are Werewolves?

2. Brad Steiger, *The Werewolf Book*. Farmington Hills, MI: Visible Ink, 1999, p. 20.
3. Sabine Baring-Gould, *The Book of Were-Wolves*, chap. 4. London: Smith, Elder, 1865, Internet Sacred Text Archive. www.sacred-texts.com.
4. Quoted in Leslie A. Sconduto, *Metamorphoses of the Werewolf: A Literary Study from Antiquity Through the Renaissance*. Jefferson, NC: McFarland, 2008, p. 36.
5. Quoted in Montague Summers, *Werewolf*. Whitefish, MT: Kessinger, 2003, p. 111.
6. Daniel Cohen, *Werewolves*. New York: Cobblehill Books, 1996, p. 6.
7. Cohen, *Werewolves*, p. 6.
8. Quoted in Robert Curran, *The Werewolf Handbook*. Hauppage, NY: Barrons Educational Series, 2010, p. 15.
9. Quoted in Steiger, *The Werewolf Book*, pp. 258–59.

Chapter Two: Encounters with Werewolves

10. Whitley Stokes, ed., *"Cóir Anmann (Fitness of Names),"* in *Irische Texte*, ed. Whitley Stokes and Ernst Windisch. Leipzig, Germany: S. Hirzel, 1897, Corpus of Electronic Texts. http://celt.ucc.ie/index.html.
11. Baring-Gould, *The Book of Were-Wolves*, chap. 4.
12. Steiger, *The Werewolf Book*, p. 28.
13. Cohen, *Werewolves*, p. 36.
14. Montague Summers, *The Werewolf*. New York: E.P. Dutton, 1934.
15. Baring-Gould, *The Book of Were-Wolves*, chapter 6.

16. Baring-Gould, *The Book of Were-Wolves*, chapter 6.

17. Baring-Gould, *The Book of Were-Wolves*, chapter 7.

18. Ed and Lorraine Warren, "Bill Ramsey the Werewolf," Ed and Lorraine Warren: The Original Ghosthunters, April 19, 2011. edandlorrainewarren.com.

19. *Weekly World News*, "A Werewolf's Chilling Story—in His Own Words!" September 3, 1991, p. 40.

20. *Weekly World News*, "A Werewolf's Chilling Story," p. 40-41

21. Katmandu, "Frequently Asked Questions for alt.horror.were wolves," Raven's Page, May 21, 2006. www.firelion.org/raven/ahwwfaq.

22. Katmandu, "Frequently Asked Questions for alt.horror.were wolves."

23. Quoted in Steiger, *The Werewolf Book*, p. 161.

24. Quoted in Steiger, *The Werewolf Book*, p. 162.

25. Franklin Ruehl, introduction to *The Werewolf Book*, by Steiger, p. ix.

Chapter Three: Werewolves in Literature and Film

26. Ovid, *Metamorphoses*, bk. 1, trans. A.S. Kline, Poetry in Translation, 2000. www.poetryintranslation.com.

27. Robert Louis Stevenson, *The Strange Case of Dr. Jekyll and Mr. Hyde, and Other Stories*. New York: Penguin Books, 1979, p. 61.

28. Guy Endore, *The Werewolf of Paris*, chap. 9. New York: Farrar & Rinehart, 1933. http://ebookbrowse, ebookbrowse.com.

29. Endore, *The Werewolf of Paris*, chap. 12.

30. Brian Linder, et al., "Top 25 Harry Potter Characters," IGN Movies, July 12, 2011. http://movies.ign.com.

31. Noel Clay, "*The Werewolf of London* (1935)," Werewolf Movies, 2007. www.werewolf-movies.com.

32. Clay, "*The Werewolf of London* (1935)."

33. Steiger, *The Werewolf Book*, p. xix.

34. Brian J. Hay, "A Collection Worth Having," Amazon.com review, October 30, 2005. www.amazon.com/review/R240EJ5WA H7VKP.

35. Grolyn, comments section, *"An American Werewolf in London,"* Upcoming Horror Movies, January 10, 2010. www.upcoming horrormovies.com.

36. BigFatOgre, comments section, *"An American Werewolf in London,"* Upcoming Horror Movies, March 17, 2011. www.upcom inghorrormovies.com.

Chapter Four: Werewolves in Popular Culture

37. CountChoculatte, "Fruit Brute! The First One!" commercial, YouTube, July 19, 2009. www.youtube.com.

38. Sonicdrivein, "Blazin' BBQ Loaded Burger-Wolfman Commercial," commercial, YouTube, May 21, 2011. www.youtube.com.

39. Adam Rosenberg, "Guillermo del Toro's Awesome Werewolf Commercial," Spinoff Online, January 3, 2011. http://spinoff .comicbookresources.com.

40. Warren Zevon, "Werewolves of London," *Excitable Boy*. Asylum Records, 1978. LP.

41. Quoted in Nina Correa, "Waddy Wachtel: Creating 'Werewolves of London,'" Waddy Wachtel, 2008. www.waddywachtelinfo .com.

42. Creedence Clearwater Revival, "Bad Moon Rising," *Green River*. Fantasy, 1969. LP.

43. Quoted in Marc Lee, "Michael Jackson's Thriller, Interview with Director John Landis," *Telegraph*, June 26, 2009. www.telegraph .co.uk.

44. White Wolf, "Old World of Darkness Wiki," August 1, 2011. http://wiki.white-wolf.com. 45. Mr. Bill and Lela, *"The Beast Within: A Gabriel Knight Mystery,"* Mr. Bill's Adventureland Review, April 2000. www.mrbillsadventureland.com.

46. Quoted in Cannibal6661, "Chupacabra Promo!!," YouTube, August 27, 2010. www.youtube.com.

For Further Exploration

Books

Sabine Baring-Gould, *The Book of Were-Wolves*. Minneola, NY: Dover Publications, 2006.

Bob Curran, *Werewolves: A Field Guide to Shapeshifters, Lycanthropes, and Man-Beasts*. Franklin Lakes, NJ: New Page Books, 2009.

Stuart A. Kallen, *Werewolves*. San Diego: ReferencePoint, 2010.

James Lowder, *Curse of the Full Moon: A Werewolf Anthology*. Berkeley, CA: Ulysses Press, 2010.

John Skipp, *Werewolves and Shape Shifters: Encounters with the Beasts Within*. New York: Black Dog & Leventhal Publishers, 2010.

Brad Steiger, *The Werewolf Book: The Encyclopedia of Shape-Shifting Beings*. Farmington Hills, MI: Visible Ink, 2011.

Serena Valentino, *How to Be a Werewolf: The Claws-On Guide for the Modern Lycanthrope*. Somerville, MA: Candlewick, 2011.

Websites

Monster Librarian (www.monsterlibrarian.com). This site offers reviews and information on horror books of all types, along with many good articles and author interviews.

Monstrous (www.monstrous.com). This site has extensive information on every imaginable monster, including werewolves.

Project Gutenberg (www.gutenberg.org). This Web site offers free full-text versions of more than 100,000 classic works, including Sabine Baring-Gould's werewolf book.

Werewolf Movies (www.werewolf-movies.com). This site offers a comprehensive, searchable database of werewolf movies and television shows from all eras.

The Werewolf Page (www.werewolfpage.com). This site is an excellent collection of resources on many different werewolf-related topics.

The Werewolf's Guide to Life (www.werewolfguidetolife.com). This site offers information for the new werewolf and also features an informative blog that focuses on werewolf topics. It is a companion page to the book of the same name.

Index

Note: Boldface page numbers indicate illustrations.

Picture Credits

About the Author

Kris Hirschmann has written more than 200 books for children. She owns and runs a business that provides a variety of writing and editorial services. She lives just outside Orlando, Florida, with her husband, Michael, and her daughters, Nikki and Erika.